USA TODAY A GANNETT COMPANY **TEEN WISE GUIDES**

TIME, MONEY, AND RELATIONSHIPS

RELATIONSHIP
SMARTS

How to Navigate Dating, Friendships, Family Relationships, and More

JOYCE MARKOVICS

TWENTY-FIRST CENTURY BOOKS / MINNEAPOLIS

Twenty-First Century Books
A division of Lerner Publishing Group, Inc.
241 First Avenue North
Minneapolis, MN 55401 U.S.A.

Website address: www.lernerbooks.com

Library of Congress Cataloging-in-Publication Data

Markovics, Joyce L.
    Relationship Smarts: How to Navigate Dating, Friendships, Family Relationships, and More / by Joyce Markovics.
        p. cm. — (USA TODAY teen wise guides: time, money, and relationships)
    Includes bibliographical references and index.
    ISBN 978-0-7613-7018-5 (lib. bdg. : alk. paper)
    1. Interpersonal relations in adolescence—Juvenile literature. 2. Friendship in adolescence—Juvenile literature.
3. Teenagers—Juvenile literature. I. Title.
BF724.3.I58M37 2012
158.2'50835—dc22   2011011849

Manufactured in the United States of America
1 – PP – 12/31/11

The images in this book are used with the permission of: © Hill Street Studios/Matthew Palmer/Blend Images/Getty Images, p. 4; © Image Source/Getty Images, pp. 5, 29, 48–49, 58; © iStockphoto.com/Jacob Wackerhausen, p. 6; © Nancy Ney/Photodisc/Getty Images, pp. 6–7, 32; © iStockphoto.com/Nicholas Homrich, p. 7; © Bellurget Jean Louis/StockImage/Getty Images, p. 8; © Stockbyte/Getty Images, p. 9; © Kevin Dodge/CORBIS, p. 10; © Radius Images/Getty Images, p. 11; © Tim Pannell/Corbis, p. 13; © iStockphoto.com/Kevin Russ, p. 14; © Jupiterimages/Brand X Pictures/Getty Images, pp. 15, 36, 40; © Ajax/CORBIS, p. 16; © iStockphoto.com/Helder Almeida, pp. 16–17; © Justin Kase Conder/USA TODAY, p. 18; © Blasius Erlinger/Stone/Getty Images, p. 19; © David Davis/Dreamstime.com, p. 20; © John Zich/USA TODAY, p. 23; © Jon Feingersh/Blend Images/Getty Images, p. 24; © age fotostock/SuperStock, pp. 25, 53; © ColorBlind Images/Iconica/Getty Images, p. 26; © Flirt/SuperStock, pp. 27, 39; © Thinkstock/Comstock Images/Getty Images, p. 30; © vario images GmbH & Co.KG/Alamy, pp. 30–31; © Ryan McVay/Photodisc/Getty Images, p. 33; © Lisa Peardon/Taxi/Getty Images, p. 35; © Picture Partners/Alamy, p. 37; © Paul Simcock/CORBIS, p. 41; © iStockphoto.com/Ryan Lane, p. 43; © Anne Barber/Alamy, p. 45; © BlueMoon Images/BlueMoon Stock/Photolibrary, p. 46; © iStockphoto.com/Andrea Haase, p. 47; © E. Dygas/Taxi/Getty Images, p. 48; © Jim Varney/Photo Researchers, Inc., p. 51; © J. Michael Short, AP Photo/USA TODAY, p. 52; © S. Kuttig/plainpicture/CORBIS, p. 55; © Thiago DaCosta/Real Latino Images/Photolibrary, p. 56; © Laurence Mouton/PhotoAlto Agency RF Collections/Getty Images, p. 57.
Front Cover: © Ross Anania/Taxi/Getty Images.

Main body text set in Conduit ITC Std 11/15
Typeface provided by International Typeface Corp

CONTENTS

INTRODUCTION
A RELATIONSHIP-FREE WORLD
4

CHAPTER 1
WHAT ARE RELATIONSHIPS?
6

CHAPTER 2
DEVELOPING RELATIONSHIPS
16

CHAPTER 3
HANDLING RELATIONSHIP QUESTIONS AND ISSUES
30

CHAPTER 4
WHEN A RELATIONSHIP TURNS BAD
48

EPILOGUE
BECOMING A RELATIONSHIP PRO
58

GLOSSARY 60
SOURCE NOTES 61
SELECTED BIBLIOGRAPHY 61
FURTHER READING 62
INDEX 64

INTRODUCTION
A RELATIONSHIP-FREE *World*

Picture this: Your cell phone chimes at six thirty in the morning, telling you it's time to get up. You throw on your favorite jeans and stagger to the kitchen for a bowl of Crunchy Os, but the normally boisterous breakfast table is a ghost town. When you arrive at school, there are no friendly faces to greet you nor any familiar chatter about the day's anticipated events. You search for your best friend to gossip about your science teacher's unfortunate slipup in class yesterday and to get advice about your upcoming dream date, but she's nowhere to be found—and neither is your love interest.

A world without relationships would be lonely and boring. What if you had to sit in the school lunchroom all by yourself?

What's going on? You've entered a relationship-free world. And while it may be less dramatic than a world filled with parents, siblings, crushes, and friends, it's also incredibly lonely. Not to mention mind-numbingly dull. Just think what life would be like if you didn't have anyone to chat idly with, spend time with, or share your innermost thoughts with. Would you feel happy and fulfilled? Probably not.

The truth is, we all need relationships. Humans are social by nature. Our need to feel connected with others is a critical part of who we are. Yet relationships can be complicated. On some days, navigating life with friends and loved ones can seem more difficult than summiting Mount Everest in flip-flops (and not the ones with fleecy insoles). This is particularly true during the teenage years—a time of life when everyone's struggling to figure out who they are and what they want out of relationships.

Fortunately, this book is here to help. It's chock-full of tips and info on establishing healthy relationships, making informed relationship decisions, and handling sticky relationship issues. So come on in! And don't hesitate to share your findings with someone you care about. Remember: we're all on this relationship journey together.

1 WHAT ARE *Relationships?*

The bonds we have with friends and other people in our lives are extremely important to our well-being.

*Y*ou may not think a ton about relationships. But they pretty much define your life. Relationships connect two or more people, such as a father and a daughter or two best friends, in some key way. Yet there's more to relationships than that. In fact, they're really complex and just as diverse as the people you know and love in your own life. For example, the connection between people in a relationship can be low-key or pretty intense, short-term or long-term, sexual or nonsexual. Many people in relationships feel passionately about one another. Others have a more casual connection.

A relationship can be other things too. It can be a series of experiences. Or a situation involving a huge group of people. Think about your family's relationship with the next-door neighbors with all the yapping dogs—or with the people on your block, on your cul-de-sac, or in your apartment building. The bottom line is that social bonds of all kinds are immensely important. They affect our lives each and every day.

YAP!
YAP!
YAP!

THE BASICS

We know that relationships are important, but do we know why that is, exactly? It comes down to what we said before about humans being naturally social. Unlike some animals—such as giant slugs and three-toed sloths—*we are not solitary creatures.* We do best when we are close to other people and when we live in social groups.

Human beings naturally seek out bonds with others.

What's more, we depend on other people to meet a lot of our emotional needs. Needs, of course, vary from person to person. But there are a couple of basics that we all have in common.

All people—no matter their gender, class, race, or religion—need to feel loved and accepted. A person who feels loved and accepted is more likely to feel good about himself or herself. We also all need to feel respected. *Everyone deserves to be respected.* While a huge variety of relationships exist, respect is a common factor in all the good ones.

RELATIONSHIP TYPES

Love, acceptance, and respect are all great things to have in a relationship. Yet no one relationship can meet all our needs, even if it has these things going for it. Family, friends, love interests, and acquaintances can all bring different perspectives and experiences to our lives. For that reason, it's normal and healthy for us to look to different types of relationships to meet our needs.

What different types of relationships can we have with other people? Although every relationship is unique, most of them do fall into a few broad groups.

FAMILY RELATIONSHIPS

The first type of relationship—and probably one of the most important—is the family relationship. The whole idea of a family group dates back millions of years. But as human society has developed and become more complex, so has the definition of family.

Starting with the most conventional description, a family can be made up of a mother, a father, brothers, sisters, and other relatives who live together. Relatives we may not live with, such as grandparents, aunts, uncles, and cousins, are also a part of our family.

This family enjoys one another's company.

USA TODAY
Life
SECTION D
LIFE.USATODAY.COM

HAVING A SISTER
IS HEALTHY, STUDY FINDS

By Stephanie Steinberg

Sisters can fend off ex-boyfriends, mean gossip and, apparently, depression. Having a sister protects teens "from feeling lonely, unloved, guilty, self-conscious and fearful," according to a study in the *Journal of Family Psychology*.

Researchers from Brigham Young University [BYU] in 2007 and 2008 studied 395 Seattle families with two or more children. They found that affectionate siblings have positive influences on each other no matter their age, gender or how many years they are apart. They promote behaviors such as kindness and generosity and protect against delinquency [unacceptable behavior or wrongdoing] and depression, says Laura Padilla-Walker, assistant professor in BYU's School of Family Life. And having a sister, rather than a brother, prevents depression, maybe because girls are better at talking about problems or are more likely to take on a caregiver role, Padilla-Walker says.

The study also found that siblings have twice as much influence as parents over performing good deeds—including volunteering, doing favors for others and being nice to people. "Siblings matter even more than parents do in terms of promoting being kind and generous," she says.

But brothers and sisters who exhibit hostility to each other are more likely to show aggressive behaviors in other relationships, says James Harper, BYU professor in the School of Family Life. "Siblings are people that a child lives with every day, and yet we haven't really seriously considered their influence," he says.

The researchers say sibling influence was stronger in families with two parents than one. A child with a single parent may become a "parent figure" to a younger sibling, Padilla-Walker says.

—August 3, 2010

Studies have shown that having a sibling—especially a sister—has significant health benefits.

We often share beliefs and values with our families, which can strengthen our emotional connection with them.

A broader and more inclusive definition of family takes nontraditional families into account. Most modern families are nontraditional. For example, many teens have parents who are separated or divorced. The children of divorced parents may divide their time between two households, depending on the custody agreement (the legal

USA TODAY Snapshots®

How U.S. divorce rate compares
Divorces per 1,000 population ages 15-64 compared with other industrial nations:

USA ■■■■■■ 6.2
United Kingdom ■■■■ 4
Sweden ■■■■ 3.8
Germany ■■■ 3.5
Canada ■■■ 3.4
France ■■■ 3.1
Japan ■■■ 3.1
Italy ■ 1

Source: U.S. Census Bureau, *Statistical Abstract of the United States, 1980-2000*

By Mark Pearson and Alejandro Gonzalez, USA TODAY, 2005

Divorce is extremely common in the United States. In fact, as this USA TODAY Snapshot shows, there are about 6.2 divorces among every one thousand people ages fifteen to sixty-four in the United States.

agreement about who has the right to take care of a child). Other teens have a single parent who has never been married. Still others have gay, lesbian, or transgendered parents. A family can also include people who are not related at all but who love and care for one another. Many families include adopted children.

No matter what type of family we come from, our families ideally love and accept us for who we are. They nurture our self-esteem and help us develop a positive image of ourselves. Of course, no family

TWO MOMS, TWO DAUGHTERS

Ry and Cade, two grown sisters from New York, were raised by two lesbian moms. They enjoyed a stable home life and a happy childhood. Their parents had a strong relationship and were always there to support their daughters. At times, however, Ry and Cade's family had to deal with discrimination. They sometimes encountered homophobia (fear or dislike of homosexuals) when they went out together as a family. "My parents [would] just hold hands and they'd get funny looks," remembered Ry.

Despite the challenges, Ry and Cade wouldn't change a thing about their parents. "You know, the older I get, the more I want to live up to what they have," Ry said. Both sisters learned that regardless of whether your parents are gay or straight, what matters is how much love a family has.

is perfect. And many teens come from families who can't meet their emotional needs due to marital conflicts, physical or mental health issues, or other serious problems. Teens in this situation might turn to friends, neighbors, clergy, or other trusted people outside their families to help meet needs not met at home.

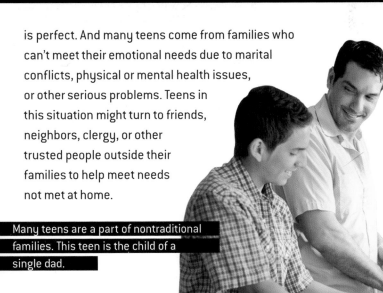

Many teens are a part of nontraditional families. This teen is the child of a single dad.

FRIENDSHIPS

Friendships are another type of relationship that can have a big influence on our lives. Friends are people we know well and with whom we form a close connection. Friends often share similar backgrounds and common interests.

Good friends give us love and support during hard times. In times of need, a simple phone call from a friend might help you regain your confidence or see something positive in a bad situation. Friends also celebrate with us in good times. If you make it into show choir or get an A on a difficult test, they're first in line to offer you their hugs and congratulations.

CASUAL RELATIONSHIPS

Casual relationships are different from family relationships and friendships. People generally have casual relationships with people they don't know very well and may see only occasionally. Have you ever started up a conversation with someone you've met only a few times or made small talk with the mail carrier who shuffles by your home every afternoon?

Casual relationships usually don't require a whole lot of effort to maintain. But a friendly chat with a casual acquaintance can brighten your day and leave you with a positive feeling. In addition, relationships with casual acquaintances can sometimes grow over time. You never know: that new kid you say hi to in the hallway between classes might one day become your best friend—or even your future prom date!

ROMANTIC RELATIONSHIPS

Romantic relationships may be the most exciting (think butterflies in your stomach), but they can also be pretty bumpy and the hardest to maintain. Romantic relationships involve an intimate emotional connection with another person. That intimacy can sometimes be physical as well, but not always.

Good romantic relationships provide us with love, close companionship, and a sense of well-being. They can make us feel that we're connected to something larger than ourselves. Yet this type of relationship takes a lot of work. There's give and take involved in any romantic relationship. Having a romantic partner means compromising, communicating, and having realistic expectations of the other person.

STAYING HEALTHY AND BALANCED

The teen years can be socially challenging, and relationships of all types can change frequently. The important thing to keep in mind is that whatever kind of relationship you're involved in, it should be healthy and balanced and allow you to grow as an individual.

These teens are just beginning a romantic relationship. Such relationships require compromise and sharing.

15

2 DEVELOPING Relationships

Meeting new people can sometimes take some effort—but just remember that even your closest friends were strangers at one point!

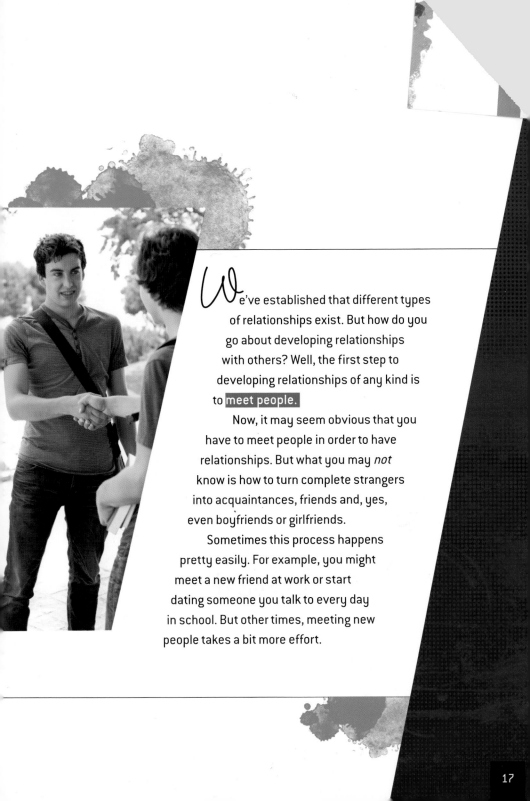

We've established that different types of relationships exist. But how do you go about developing relationships with others? Well, the first step to developing relationships of any kind is to meet people.

Now, it may seem obvious that you have to meet people in order to have relationships. But what you may *not* know is how to turn complete strangers into acquaintances, friends and, yes, even boyfriends or girlfriends.

Sometimes this process happens pretty easily. For example, you might meet a new friend at work or start dating someone you talk to every day in school. But other times, meeting new people takes a bit more effort.

MEET YOU AT THE BALLPARK!

For those times when social contacts don't just fall into your lap—or for times when you just want to expand your social circle—*getting involved in activities is a great thing to try.* In addition to helping us meet people, activities can expose us to new experiences and help us learn new skills.

Sports are one activity that you could get involved in. Maybe you could try out for your school's baseball team or join a community soccer league. If sports aren't your thing, you could consider volunteering. Talk to your school's guidance counselor or a community leader about opportunities to volunteer at a local senior center, hospital, or humane society. Theater groups, book clubs, and debate teams can also offer opportunities to make new friends. Even going for a jog through your neighborhood or taking your dog for a walk can lead to meeting someone new.

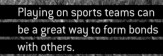

Playing on sports teams can be a great way to form bonds with others.

ONLINE CONNECTIONS

Another way to get to know people is by visiting social networking sites and Internet chat rooms. The Internet provides countless opportunities to meet and communicate with people around the world. Many chat rooms are organized around sports, music, or other topics, so you can get to know people with common interests.

Make sure not to give out too much information about yourself when you meet people online. Stay safe by talking to an adult if you are considering meeting an online friend in person.

However, if you're going to socialize online, there are a few things to be aware of. First of all, when you're surfing the Internet or chatting with a new "e-friend," you should never reveal personal information about yourself, such as your full name, address, phone number, passwords, or any financial information. People you meet online may not always be who they say they are. Someone who seems friendly might really just be out to steal info they can use to break into your bank account or make fraudulent purchases in your name.

Second, you should be extremely cautious about agreeing to meet your online friends in person. If you feel you really want to meet an online friend, make sure to get a parent's permission first. If your parent approves of the meeting, meet the person in a public place and bring the parent or another trusted adult with you. (The adult doesn't actually have to be standing there when you meet your friend, but he or she should be nearby just in case.) Since people on the Internet aren't always who they seem, you can never be too careful. You'll want to have a safe way out in case the person you were chatting with turns out to be a sexual predator or someone else with bad intentions.

Finally, if you ever have an uncomfortable experience online, such as being threatened or bullied, *tell someone!* You can start by telling administrators of the website on which the bullying took place. Teachers, parents, your school's technology specialist, and other adults can help you deal with the situation too. Telling an adult might also save another teen from going through the same ordeal.

USA TODAY Snapshots®

Scared at school

Percentage of students ages 12-18 who were bullied at school during the previous six months, by location of bullying:

Inside school **79%**

Outside on school grounds **28%**

School bus **8%**

Somewhere else **5%**

Source: Department of Education

By David Stuckey and Alejandro Gonzalez, USA TODAY, 2006

Most young people are bullied at one time or another—whether at school, on the school bus, or on the Internet. This USA TODAY Snapshot shows the prevalence of bullying.

CYBERBULLYING
GROWS BIGGER AND MEANER

By Janet Kornblum

Ricky, a high school student from Lake County, Indiana, doesn't know which classmate [secretly] hoisted a cellphone camera and snapped his picture or exactly when it happened. All Ricky, 16, knows is the fuzzy yet distinguishable portrait of him in English class showed up on MySpace, on a page that claimed to be his. And the fake profile, titled "The Rictionary," not only identified his school but also said Ricky loved dictionaries—a swipe at his school smarts—and was gay (he's not), one of the most common schoolyard taunts. "I was completely devastated," Ricky says.

As younger and more kids get their hands on cellphone and digital cameras and high-speed Internet connections, cyberbullying is ramping up and taking new forms. No longer are threats, taunts and insults relegated [being left] to the written word in chat rooms and instant messages. Now teens, children and sometimes adults are adding pictures and videos to their bullying arsenal and posting them on sites such as MySpace, Facebook and YouTube, where anyone can see them.

And bullying has led to real consequences—from fights to teen suicides, or what some label "bullycides." States are beginning to take action with tough new laws targeting those who use electronic means to bully.

Compounding the frustration is that children often fail to report bullying. They fear that tormentors will become angrier and bully them more or worry that if they report being bullied over the Internet or on a cellphone, their phone and Internet privileges will be revoked.

"You're bullied twice," says Nancy Willard, author of *Cyber-Safe Kids, Cyber-Savvy Teens* and *Cyberbullying and Cyberthreats*. "You're bullied in the real world with a physical attack, and then you're bullied on-line with humiliation. It's very hurtful. Cyberbullying can be even more destructive [than face-to-face bullying] because you get a sense that the whole world is being exposed to what is being said to you."

That's just how Ricky feels. "When they put it on the Internet, it's like they

Ricky and his mother, Peggy, tend to cows on their farm. Ricky was the victim of cyberbullying when someone created a fake MySpace profile in his name.

took everything and multiplied it," he says. "When you put it on the Internet, you are opening it up to everyone."

Ricky called his mother the spring day he discovered the profile and had her pick him up from school. He didn't have many friends to begin with. But soon he found himself more alone than ever.

"I had thought about suicide," he says. "It looked very welcoming at certain times." But he says his family is helping him cope.

His mother, Peggy, 44, tells her son he just has to make it through two more years of high school. But she's worried. "Does it hurt him forever? You bet. Ricky has been crushed."

In the past few months, Peggy has done everything she could think of to remedy the situation. MySpace eventually removed the profile—only after several weeks of pestering the site, she says. Other than that, "everybody is passing the buck."

Mike Chelap, assistant vice principal of the high school Ricky attends, says he can't discuss personal matters about students, but the school began an anti-bullying program and will implement it in the fall.

—July 15, 2008

GETTING CHATTY

Another way to get to know people is by simply being warm and friendly. Try talking with people, from the older woman down the block who works in her garden every day to the guy who sits next to you in science class. Anytime you talk to someone, you have a chance at making a new friend.

Remember to keep your conversation positive. No one likes someone who complains all the time. Making eye contact and smiling is also a great way to connect with others.

Not sure what to say? Try complimenting the other person. Or make a comment about your environment. It's something that you and the other person both share in common. The weather is a classic conversation starter for a reason! You could also ask for advice or help with something, such as hanging posters to promote a neighborhood cleanup day or completing a particularly tricky homework assignment.

Not every conversation is going to result in a friendship. And be smart about who you talk to . But even if you strike up a conversation with someone you never talk to again, you will have had a positive exchange. It just may make the day a little better for both you and the other person.

RELATIONSHIP BUILDING 101

Now that you know how to increase your social contacts, let's look at some ways to build your relationships—both the ones you have already and the ones you'll have in the future. Building your relationships helps them grow stronger. It deepens your connection with the people you love and care about.

One of the most important things you can do to build your relationships is to—you guessed it!—communicate. We all know the importance of talking. However, good communication is much more than a casual "Hey, what's up?" in the hallway or shooting the breeze between bites during lunch.

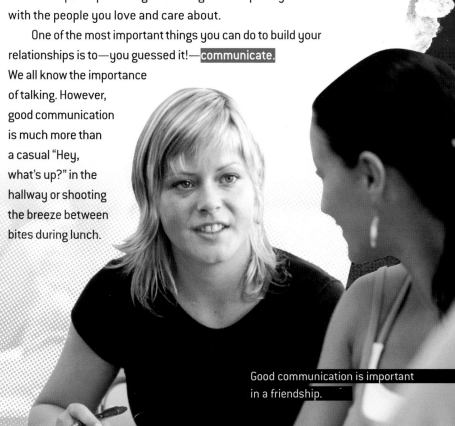

Good communication is important in a friendship.

To build relationships, you have to talk openly and honestly and express your true feelings. Good communication in a personal relationship means not being afraid to say what's on your mind and not limiting what you say to things you think the other person wants to hear. People who communicate in an open manner are more likely to avoid miscommunication, which can lead to trouble down the road.

LISTEN UP

Another essential part of relationship building is knowing when to close your mouth and open your ears. Listening is at least as important as talking in a relationship. Being a good listener involves taking the time to let someone express himself or herself. Sometimes it takes a while for a person to think about what he or she wants to say. A good listener has a lot of patience and understanding and won't pressure someone to talk when he or she isn't ready to.

Listening is a crucial part of building any relationship.

Nonverbal cues also come into play when it comes to listening. Eye contact—that all-important staple of good communication—lets people know that you're paying attention. Leaning forward slightly and mirroring the other person's posture and gestures are also subtle signs of attentiveness. When you mirror someone else's body language, it shows that you're in tune with him or her. Just don't parrot everything the other person does. *That can come across as creepy rather than attentive!*

A SHOULDER TO CRY ON

Yet another key in building good relationships is to be there for the other person. Have you ever had a friend who stood by your side when things were going really well but bailed on you when life got stressful? Support among friends shouldn't be conditional. No matter the circumstances, you and your friend should always be there for each other. We usually need the most support when we're faced with a difficult situation, such as an ill family member or a messy breakup. A supportive person knows how to listen and can express empathy (sympathy and understanding) when you're down.

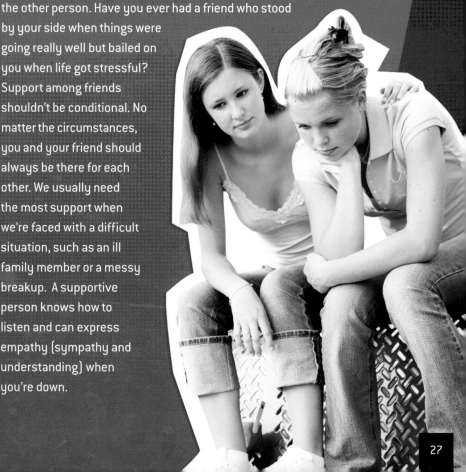

A RELATIONSHIP BALANCING ACT

Balance is still another relationship-building must. Balance exists in a relationship when each person contributes equally. One person shouldn't call all the shots while the other person struggles to be heard. Rather, both people should work together for the benefit of each other and their relationship.

WHAT DO YOU THINK OF YOURSELF?

The last—but certainly not the least—element in building a healthy relationship has to do with your self-image. Self-image is a kind of mental picture we have of ourselves, including how we look and act. Our self-image begins to form at a very young age and changes over time. It can be positive, negative, or a combination of both.

DID YOU KNOW?

According to health experts, having healthy relationships with others can actually benefit your physical health. A number of medical studies have shown that:

- people with strong social connections live longer than those who do not.
- people who are engaged in healthy relationships have stronger immune systems, which helps our bodies fight disease.
- people who have strong social connections have lower blood pressure than people who don't. High blood pressure can lead to heart disease and other medical problems.
- the endocrine and cardiovascular systems (the glands and the heart and blood vessels) are healthier in people with lots of close friends.

Self-image is pretty crucial when it comes to being in a relationship. Why? Because your self-image is tied into how much you feel loved, accepted, and respected by yourself and others. People with poor self-images often feel as if no one will truly like them for who they are. Those with positive self-images, on the other hand, feel good about themselves and tend to have an optimistic view about relationships.

To have great relationships with other people, you must first have a great relationship with yourself. Many people feel uncertain about who they are during their teenage years, which is a completely normal part of adolescence. However, even as your sense of identity fluctuates, know that you are an individual with value. Not feeling good about who you are can make it hard to develop a meaningful connection with others.

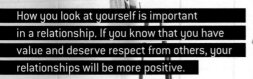

How you look at yourself is important in a relationship. If you know that you have value and deserve respect from others, your relationships will be more positive.

3 HANDLING RELATIONSHIP
Questions and Issues

Sometimes people fight, argue, and disagree. But there are things you can do to make your relationships better.

$\mathcal{E}$ven if you have good communication skills, unconditional support, balance, and a healthy self-image going for you in most of your relationships, interactions with others can still be tricky. Close relationships often come with a lot of issues and emotions. These can be difficult to deal with at times. Yet whether you're facing parental problems, fickle friendships, or dating dilemmas, there are steps you can take to better the situation. So read on, and know that all is not lost!

FAMILY DRAMA

Family life is nothing like a TV sitcom. If anything, it's more like a reality TV show—only a lot less fake. *Relationships at home can be complicated* and confusing for teenagers and can result in many arguments. A big part of the reason for this is that as teens move toward adulthood, they want more freedom and the ability to make decisions about their own lives. Yet parents often have rules that limit what you do, where you go, and who you spend time with. These rules can seem to challenge your desire for independence.

What actions can you take when parental rules feel stifling? And what can you do to help keep the peace at home? One thing you might try is to discuss household rules with your parents. You can explain how the rules affect you and then ask to hear their side about why the rules exist. Make sure to talk calmly and listen respectfully to what they have to say. If your parents are open to further discussion, you could explain how you think the rules could be changed or improved. Your parents just might be willing to change a rule—such as not permitting you to go out on a school night or to get a car—if you make your points in a mature and thoughtful fashion.

Parents and teenagers can disagree on rules. Some teens want more freedom than their parents are willing to give.

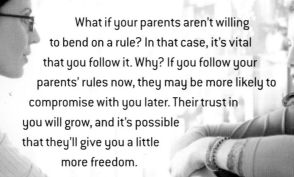

What if your parents aren't willing to bend on a rule? In that case, it's vital that you follow it. Why? If you follow your parents' rules now, they may be more likely to compromise with you later. Their trust in you will grow, and it's possible that they'll give you a little more freedom.

Following your parents' rules can help them to trust you more. If you screw up and don't follow your parents' rules, take time out to apologize.

APOLOGIZE . . . AND GRACE YOUR PARENTS WITH YOUR PRESENCE

Another piece of advice to follow when you're dealing with your family is to apologize when you mess up in some way. This might include as overreacting to a parent's request to clean your room or making a nasty comment to your brother. Taking the time to acknowledge that you've screwed up will show that you're mature. It will also go a long way toward gaining your family's trust.

Spending time together as a family can also improve family relationships. Family members sometimes drift apart because everyone's so involved in his or her own life. But if you carve out time to do things with your family, you'll see what a difference spending time together makes. You may even want to initiate an activity, such as going to a theme park or seeing the latest blockbuster movie.

Although family relationships can be sticky in the teen years, *your family is one of the cornerstones of your life.* Giving your time, love, and attention to your family is one of the best investments you can make.

FRIEND TODAY, GONE TOMORROW

Like family relationships, friendships can be tumultuous in the teen years. They sometimes turn from great to complicated—or even just plain rotten—in what seems like the blink of an eye.

One reason that friendships can be rocky in your teens is that there's a *lot* of pressure to fit in. Peer pressure can wear on us as well as strain our relationships. If you've ever felt pressured to do something that you knew was wrong or that you just didn't want to do, such as making fun of someone or having sex because your friends did, then you know how much discomfort peer pressure can cause. *Even subtle peer pressure can cause stress.* For example, maybe all your friends have smartphones and expensive MP$_3$ players, so you feel you should have them too—even though you know you can't afford them.

What do you do when peer pressure rears its ugly head? How do you balance your desire to fit in with the need to do what's right for you? Every situation is different, but there are a few helpful tricks you can try.

If you know you're going into a situation where you're likely to face peer pressure, *think ahead about how you want to handle things.* Come up with a good reason or two to help explain why you don't want to do what others are doing. For example, let's say you're going to a party where you think you might be offered alcohol or drugs. You could explain that you have a big game coming up and that you don't want to mess up your performance by drinking or using. Or you could say that you've been interviewing for jobs and don't want to risk failing an employer's drug test. Of course, true friends shouldn't question you if you just tell them that you're not comfortable consuming alcohol or drugs. But it doesn't hurt to have a few explanations at the ready, just in case peer pressure gets intense.

It can feel awkward to go against the group when you're hanging out with friends. Having a few coping strategies at the ready can make the situation easier.

Another way to combat peer pressure is to stick close to a friend who shares your values when it comes to things like bullying, drinking, sex, and smoking. If both of you stand up together and refuse to do certain things, speaking up can suddenly feel a whole lot easier.

Finally, you could work out an "escape plan" with a parent to get yourself out of peer-pressure-filled situations. For instance, you could agree to call home and use a "code phrase"—such as, "Could you come pick me up? I'm feeling nauseated"—when you find yourself faced with lots of tough peer pressure.

FRIENDSHIPS AND CLIQUES

Cliques can also create difficulties in the teen years.

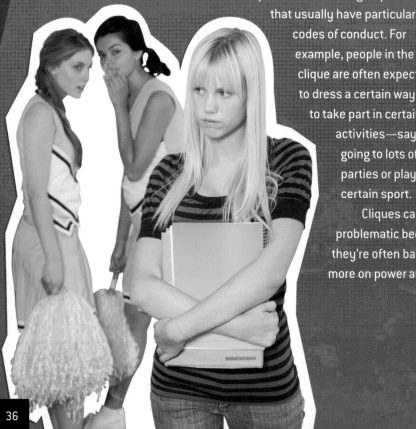

Cliques are exclusive groups of friends that usually have particular codes of conduct. For example, people in the clique are often expected to dress a certain way or to take part in certain activities—say, going to lots of parties or playing a certain sport.

Cliques can be problematic because they're often based more on power and control than on true friendship. People in the clique might use gossip or humiliation to preserve their status and to keep others out. They might do such things as spread a rumor that the new girl in school had to transfer from her old school because she was bullied—or that the guy the ringleader of the clique used to date gets nervous whenever he gives a kiss. Such stories make the clique look more powerful than the target of their gossip. They also serve to exclude the target from the clique.

If someone wants to break free of the clique and the behavior the clique embraces, he or she can sometimes run into an uncomfortable social situation. Members of the clique may start gossiping about that person or do other mean things.

SPOTLIGHT ON CONFLICT

Conflict can cause stress among friends. This is true at any stage of life, not just in the teenage years. You and your friends aren't always going to see eye to eye. But if you find yourself in a conflict, here are a few things you can try to help restore the sanity.

- Let everyone involved in the conflict express how he or she feels about it. Talking things over can go a long way toward resolving conflicts. No one should interrupt while anyone else is speaking, and everyone should agree not to criticize what others say. It's critical for everyone to get a chance to be heard.
- Make "I statements." "I statements" are statements that begin with the word *I*, such as, "I feel bad when you cancel plans with me to hang out with your friends from the hockey team instead." "I statements" are less likely to put others on the defensive than are "you statements," such as "You make me feel bad when you bail out on plans."
- Avoid name-calling and insults. Conversations can get heated when we're angry, but lashing out at others only makes a conflict worse.
- Engage in active listening. Active listening is when you listen fully and carefully to what others are saying and then repeat back what you have just heard. For example, you might say, "So you're saying you feel ignored when I don't answer your texts." This lets the other person know that you listened and gives him or her the chance to explain some more if you misunderstood.
- Put yourself in the other person's shoes. Remember that we all bring different feelings and life experiences to conflicts. Thinking about where someone else may be coming from can help you feel more compassionate toward him or her.

Feeling excluded by a clique can be hard, but there are effective ways to deal with it.

If you're in a clique—or if you've ever felt rejected or excluded by a clique—there are a few ways you can deal. First of all, whether you're on the inside or the outside of a clique, *it's important to know and have confidence in your own values.* Ask yourself if you want the clique members to accept you because you think they are (or could be) true friends or because you just feel the need to be accepted by the "cool kids." If it's the latter, the clique probably isn't the best place for you. You shouldn't sweat it too much if you find yourself on the outside. Even if the clique members tease you or spread rumors because you're not one of them, you're better off not hanging out with them just to build your social status. Besides, people who would bully or harass you aren't worth your time anyway.

Second, it can help to participate in activities that make you feel good about yourself. Don't allow people in the clique to convince you that you don't like computer programming or scrapbooking because these aren't activities that *they* enjoy. If you find these things interesting, then by all means do them! In addition to building your self-esteem, participating in activities can give you something to focus on besides whether you're in or out of the clique.

Last but not least, it's a good idea to keep your circle of friends diverse, even if it means befriending people on the outside of your usual social group. Friends who aren't in a clique can help you make social connections without worrying about being "cool." And who knows? Their opinions, interests, and behaviors just might end up being a better match for you than those of the popular crowd.

DATING DIFFICULTIES

Romantic relationships come with just as many challenges as family relationships and friendships, if not more. As exciting as they are, they don't always turn out the way the people involved might hope. Not everyone has romantic relationships in middle school or high school. But no matter what stage you're at in the dating game, learning about romantic relationships can help you as you think about maintaining or someday developing a close emotional connection with another person.

Romantic relationships can be very rewarding—but they can also be among the hardest relationships to maintain.

Romantic relationships are challenging because *so many complicated feelings are involved*. When you first feel a romantic spark with someone else, your heart may race, your stomach could churn, and your mind probably runs in a thousand different directions. You might feel as if you're in love—though at this early stage, it's really hard to see things objectively. It probably isn't *really* love just yet, as you and your romantic interest haven't had time to develop the emotional intimacy, respect, and trust that exists in a loving relationship. But nonetheless, the physical and emotional connection you feel toward your crush is probably pretty intense.

When you're wrapped up in the feelings that come with having a crush, few things can seem more exciting than the prospect of dating your love interest. You might even have high hopes that the relationship could blossom into a long-term commitment. But sometimes—even in spite of your strong feelings—things don't go as you'd imagined if you and your crush end up dating. Maybe you discover that you have little to talk about. Maybe you just don't click for one reason or another. Or maybe one of you is interested in pursuing a relationship while the other one isn't so sure.

When you and your romantic interest don't connect, it can be disappointing—especially if he or she doesn't seem as interested as you are.

When you first start dating someone, your heart may race and you might feel as if you're in love. But true love usually takes some time to develop.

41

But it can help to remember that you aren't going to click with everyone you date. Indeed, that's the whole point of dating—to find out if you and someone you're attracted to are really a good match. Besides, you'll have plenty of other opportunities to meet people. Try not to worry too much that this particular connection didn't work out.

SEX . . . OR NOT?

After some trial and error in dating, you might find someone you do connect with—someone with whom you feel a special spark and may even be in love with. If you find yourself in this situation, you might be faced with another potentially confusing relationship issue: the decision whether or not to have sex.

For some people, the choice might be clear. You may know for certain that you want to have a physical relationship with your partner, or you may know without a doubt that you want to hold off. But for other people, the decision is a little murkier.

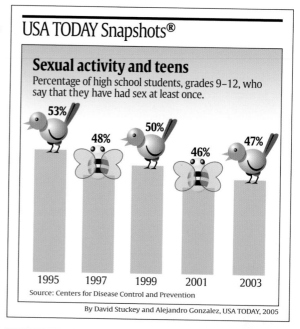

USA TODAY Snapshots®

Sexual activity and teens
Percentage of high school students, grades 9–12, who say that they have had sex at least once.

53% — 1995
48% — 1997
50% — 1999
46% — 2001
47% — 2003

Source: Centers for Disease Control and Prevention

By David Stuckey and Alejandro Gonzalez, USA TODAY, 2005

Societal messages sometimes suggest that everyone is having sex—but that's not the case. As this USA TODAY Snapshot shows, fewer than half of all high school students had had sex in three out of five years in which they were surveyed. But regardless of statistics, the important thing is to do what's best for you.

How do you know if you're ready to have sex? Everyone must use his or her own judgment in this matter, but here are a few questions that can help you think it through.

- **How do you feel about yourself?** Before you have sex, you should feel good about yourself and confident in the decisions you make.
- **How do you feel about your partner?** Ideally, your partner will be someone you trust and care about and someone you're able to confide in. The two of you should be comfortable talking openly and honestly about sex before you have a sexual relationship.
- **How much do you know about birth control?** It's important to be aware of and to use contraception—whether its condoms or diaphragms or birth control pills—if you're thinking about having sex.
- **How much do you know about safe sex and sexually transmitted diseases?** You should be a pro! Parents, health-care providers, and reliable websites can help you out here. Safe sex is a must, though it doesn't happen automatically. It requires planning and a commitment to follow through with that plan.
- **What are your personal values when it comes to sex?** The decision to have sex should feel right to you and should be in line with your values and beliefs.

No matter what you decide about sex, it's important to think carefully about what's at stake and to consider the possible repercussions. The decision to have sex isn't something to take lightly. It carries consequences that could potentially affect you for the rest of your life.

Birth control pills are one option for preventing pregnancy.

THE TRUTH ABOUT SEX:
TEEN BOYS LIE ABOUT IT

By Sharon Jayson

T eenage boys and young men may talk a lot about sex, but often the only ones listening are their peers. Now, an on-line survey of 1,200 guys ages 15 to 22 gives them a clear voice. And the girls are listening.

"Everybody thinks they just want to have sex—that it's all about getting it on," says Ann Shoket, editor in chief of *Seventeen* magazine, which commissioned the survey in partnership with the non-profit National Campaign to Prevent Teen and Unplanned Pregnancy for the magazine's March issue, out next week. "But [our findings show] they're also looking for some relationship."

Although the magazine's focus was on sexual respect, the on-line survey by TRU, a Chicago-based youth market research company, asked [boys] 42 questions about sex and relationships, including attitudes and sexual history. Among the findings:

- 45% said they were virgins.
- 60% said they had lied about something related to sex; 30% lied about how far they have gone; 24% lied about their number of sexual partners; and 23% claimed not to be a virgin when they were.
- 57% of sexually active respondents said they had had unprotected sex.
- 78% agreed there was "way too much pressure" from society to have sex.

"People watch shows like *Jersey Shore* and *Real World* or listen to music that makes it a big deal. People are surrounded by it," says Jake Helgenberg, 17, a high school junior from Paoli, Pennsylvania, who is studying ballet in New York City and was among the survey respondents.

Keenan Cooks, 19, of Boston, a sophomore studying communication arts at Marymount Manhattan College in New York City, also participated in the

Young men often talk a lot about sex—but their true feelings on the subject may be different than you think.

survey. He says guys lie about sex "to appear like they're the man—they have some type of clout [influence or power] and they're a player."

They may not be as experienced as they suggest, and, "if they are, they have to stretch it," he says. "They'll say 'experienced' to a female but not how many they've had to make her think she's special."

Other survey findings:

- 51% said having sex before marriage was acceptable in their family.
- 53% said they had had a conversation with a parent about preventing pregnancy.
- 66% said they could be happy in a serious relationship that didn't include sex.

—*January 26, 2010*

SPOTLIGHT ON SEXUAL ORIENTATION

Sexual orientation describes a person's attraction toward other people, whether of the opposite sex, the same sex, or both sexes. Sexual orientation is not something that can be changed. Rather, it is an innate part of who we are. People who are heterosexual are physically attracted to members of the opposite sex. People who are homosexual are physically attracted to people of the same sex. Bisexuals are attracted to people of both sexes.

Many homosexual teens feel pressured to hide their sexual orientation. Some heterosexual teens may bully their homosexual peers. This bullying can severely hurt the victim's self-esteem and cause emotional pain. Homosexual teens who face bullying can benefit greatly from a supportive, loving network of family and friends. Resources such as the It Gets Better Project (a website that airs videos with positive messages for gay teens) and the Born This Way Blog (a site where gay adults share childhood pictures and stories about growing up gay) can help too. These sites can be found at http://www.itgetsbetter.org and http://borngaybornthisway.blogspot.com, respectively.

Some homosexual teens experience bullying. Having support from family and friends can help.

HEARTBREAK

Another common issue in romantic relationships—and perhaps the toughest one of all to deal with—is heartbreak. *Not all romantic relationships work out.* Some end on good terms, while others feel like "epic fails." Bad communication, lots of fighting, or a relationship that's based on the wrong things (such as lust or selfishness) are some of the reasons relationships end. Whatever the reason, the feelings of loss after a breakup can be acute.

How do you cope when your heart's been broken? Getting support from friends and family or a therapist can help. Just talking things through can go a long way toward mending a broken heart. Shifting your focus is another coping strategy. Going to the movies, reading a great book, or working out are excellent distractions. Exercise can be especially helpful because it's a natural mood booster.

It's also important to eat healthfully when you're going through a breakup. Sometimes stress can make you lose your appetite—or make you want to binge on ice cream and potato chips. But whole grains, veggies, fruits, and other healthful foods will help give you energy and keep your stress in check.

As challenging as romantic relationships are, they can also be very rewarding. They help us get to know ourselves and identify what we're looking for in a partner. Give yourself time and patience when it comes to exploring the dating world, and know that everyone's path is different. There is no right or wrong. It's all about what's right for *you!*

4 WHEN A RELATIONSHIP
Turns Bad

Physical, sexual, and emotional abuse are very serious relationship issues. It's crucial for anyone facing these issues to get help.

While issues such as breakups, peer pressure, and arguments with parents are undoubtedly tough to deal with, some relationship issues are truly dire and require outside help. Abuse is one such issue.

Abuse affects many teens regardless of gender, race, sexual orientation, or class. Indeed, it can happen to anyone. Fortunately, you can take steps to protect yourself from being victimized by a boyfriend, a girlfriend, a parent, or a so-called friend.

WHAT IS ABUSE?

In basic terms, abuse is the maltreatment of another person. A lot of people mistakenly believe that abuse always leaves physical marks. But in many cases, the effects of abuse are emotional or psychological—and thus often invisible to outsiders. Abuse falls into three main categories: physical abuse, sexual abuse, and emotional abuse. An abusive relationship often involves more than one type of abuse.

PHYSICAL ABUSE

Physical abuse is the most familiar kind of abuse. It involves being physically violent toward another person and includes slapping, pushing, strangling, kicking, and punching. Physical abuse rarely stops at one attack. In fact, it often becomes more frequent over time, and the attacks may become more violent.

SEXUAL ABUSE

Sexual abuse occurs when one person forces another to engage in sexual behavior. Such behavior may include inappropriate touching, sexual intercourse, or an unwanted sexual encounter. Sexual abuse can occur in the family, in romantic relationships, and even in friendships. When it occurs in the family, it is known as incest. Both males and females can be victims of sexual abuse, but most often, females are the victims. Sometimes abuse may be the result of impaired judgment due to alcohol or drug use.

Most teen love is abuse-free

About one-quarter[1] of sexually active teens do report some abuse during their first sexual relationship:

No violence	Verbal abuse such as name-calling	Any physical, such as pushing or shoving	Both physical and verbal
74%	24%	9%	7%

1 — Percentages don't add up to 100% because groups are not mutually exclusive.
Source: Child Trends Research Brief

By Bob Laird, USA TODAY, 2000

While abuse is a pressing problem in teen relationships, the good news is that most teens aren't abused. As this USA TODAY graphic shows, 74 percent of teens report no abuse in their first sexual relationship.

This teen is afraid after being assaulted by her partner. No one deserves abuse of any kind.

EMOTIONAL ABUSE

Emotional abuse is when someone isolates, manipulates, threatens, or verbally assaults another person. Emotional abuse can also include teasing, bullying, and harassment. Over time, emotional abuse can damage the victim's self-esteem. It can even cause the victim to feel worthless or deserving of abuse. However, *no one ever deserves abuse.* The first step to getting out of an abusive relationship is to realize that you have the right to be treated with dignity and respect.

THE REALITY OF RAPE

A lot of teens think that rape happens only between two strangers. But in reality, many people who are raped know their attacker. The attacker could be an acquaintance, a friend, or even a boyfriend or a girlfriend. Rape by a boyfriend or a girlfriend is known as date rape.

A rapist may use alcohol or a date rape drug such as Rohypnol—also called roofies—to take advantage of another person. The alcohol or drug may cause the victim to lose consciousness or to become extremely confused. Then the rapist forces a sexual encounter.

A rapist may try to justify his or her actions by saying that the victim wanted sex or was asking for it by dressing or behaving suggestively. But the person who is raped is never to blame. Rape is always the rapist's fault. This is true even if the rapist and the victim have had consensual sex (sex that both people agreed to) in the past. No matter the circumstances, sex forced on another person is always rape.

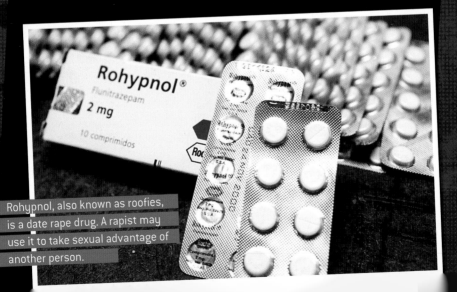

Rohypnol, also known as roofies, is a date rape drug. A rapist may use it to take sexual advantage of another person.

WARNING SIGNS OF ABUSE

How can you tell if you or a friend or a loved one is being abused? Sometimes you may know for sure. Other times, it isn't quite so clear. But if you or your friend or loved one is in a relationship with someone who does any of the following, it's a sign that it's time to get help.

- Delivers constant put-downs
- Displays controlling or dominating behavior
- Displays extreme jealousy
- Has an explosive temper
- Isolates you or your friend or loved one from family and friends
- Has big mood swings
- Is possessive
- Tries to restrict what you or your friend or loved one does

An explosive temper is one sign your partner might be abusive.

USA TODAY

Life

SECTION D

LIFE.USATODAY.COM

ABUSIVE TEEN DATING
BEHAVIOR GOES HIGH-TECH

By Sharon Jayson

A national education campaign and phone hotline to curb abusive teen dating behavior goes into effect today, prompted by new research that suggests teens and technology sometimes make for troublesome connections. The campaign launches with an interactive teen website (Loveisrespect.org) and a 24-hour hotline (866-331-9474) paid for with $1 million over three years by Liz Claiborne Inc. as part of the company's efforts to end domestic violence. The hotline will be operated by the National Domestic Violence Hotline, a 10-year-old, confidential, 24-hour service in Austin, Texas.

The research, commissioned by Claiborne, was done in December by Teenage Research Unlimited. The on-line survey of 615 young people 13 to 18 found that cellphones and the Internet make it easier for teenagers to be intimidated and emotionally abused without their parents' knowledge.

Of those surveyed, 382 said they had been in a relationship. Among those who ever had a boyfriend or girlfriend:

- 18.6% said a boyfriend or girlfriend spread rumors about them using a cellphone, e-mail, instant messaging, text, Web chat, blog or social networking site.
- 18.1% said information posted on a social networking site was used to harass or put them down.
- 24.6% said a cellphone, e-mail, instant message, Web chat or blog were used to put them down or say "really mean things."

Young people fear that no one will believe them, and they must see the person who has been controlling, manipulating or otherwise abusing them every day in school, says Sheryl Cates of the National Domestic Violence Hotline. It fields more than 18,000 calls a month; about 10% are from teenagers.

Although much dating abuse can be emotional, 2005 data from the Centers for Disease Control and Prevention show that 9% of U.S. students had been hit, slapped or physically hurt by a boyfriend or girlfriend in the previous year.

Technology can make it easier for dating abuse to take place without a parent's knowledge.

Kendrick Sledge, 19, a Boston University sophomore from Upper Arlington, Ohio, says she was in an abusive relationship in her freshman year of high school and didn't know any better. "I had no clue this was actually a problem and wasn't just happening to me," she says. It was her first relationship.

Teens often don't know how to handle intimacy and conflict because they see "very poor messages" in the media and in music videos, says David Wolfe, a professor of psychology and psychiatry at the University of Toronto. "Girls don't recognize an abusive situation," he says. "They think that's what love is: 'He's jealous and watches me closely.'"

—*February 8, 2007*

Bullying is a common form of abuse. Bullies and other abusers often have emotional problems that may require them to seek outside help.

In addition, if a friend or a loved one has bruises or other unexplained injuries, it may be a sign that abuse is taking place. When it comes to abuse, a good rule of thumb is to trust your instincts. If something in your or a friend's relationship doesn't seem right, it probably isn't.

SEEKING HELP

What should you do if you know that you or a friend is being abused? It can be difficult to end an abusive relationship, especially if that relationship is violent. No one should try to get out of an abusive relationship on his or her own. The best approach is to ask for help and support from a trusted adult.

Adults you might turn to include teachers, coaches, friends, family members, or professionals at domestic violence agencies. In cases of dating violence, the National Dating Abuse Helpline is an excellent resource. It can be reached at 1-866-331-9474 or 1-866-331-8543. Another helpline is the Childhelp National Child Abuse Hotline. In addition to victims of dating violence, it helps young people experiencing domestic abuse or abuse by a friend or an acquaintance. The number is 1-800-4-A-CHILD.

No matter to whom you turn for help, the important thing is to reach out to someone. Know that everyone deserves to feel safe and that escape from abuse is possible. Many people and resources are available to help you.

EPILOGUE
BECOMING A *Relationship Pro*

*I*f you've made it this far, you know all about the different types of relationships, how to meet people and build relationships, and how to deal with a variety of relationship issues. You're becoming a relationship pro! *But is there anything else you need to know about relationships?*

Yes! Here are just a few more pointers that will help you successfully manage life with friends, acquaintances, and loved ones. These takeaway tips can help enhance just about any kind of relationship.

- **Be honest.** If you say you're going to do something, do it. People will trust you more if your words and actions are one and the same. Also make sure to be upfront about your feelings. Don't say things that aren't true just to please people. If people find out you lied, they won't be pleased.
- **Be loyal.** Loyalty counts for a lot. So fight the temptation to gossip about friends and loved ones behind their backs, even if they've done something to upset you. And if you make plans with someone, keep them. Just because the girl you like invites you to a last-minute party doesn't mean you can ditch out on hosting gaming night with the guys.
- **Be respectful.** Know that everyone deserves to be treated with courtesy. If your parents ask you to do the dishes, don't snap at them. If a friend doesn't want to share details about her date, don't push her. Show a little respect to others, and you'll be amazed at how much you get back in return.
- **Be generous.** Pitch in if a friend asks you to help him clean out his car. Consider loaning your sister a sweater if she asks. If you make an effort to help the people in your life, they'll be more willing to help you out when you need it.
- **Be forgiving.** Don't jump to conclusions about why a friend broke a promise or was late picking you up for school. Ask the friend what happened, and then try to be understanding. Remember that nobody's perfect. We all slip up from time to time.

Most important of all, be yourself. *Value, respect, and express the true you.* Remember: Your relationships are really all about who you are!

GLOSSARY

ABUSE: the maltreatment of another person. Abuse can be physical, sexual, or emotional.

ACTIVE LISTENING: listening fully and carefully to others and repeating back what you think you heard. Active listening gives the other person a chance to explain himself or herself further and to correct any misunderstandings.

BISEXUAL: a person who is attracted to members of both the opposite sex and the same sex

CLIQUE: an exclusive group of friends that usually has a particular code of conduct

CONSENSUAL SEX: sex in which both partners are willing participants

CONTRACEPTION: birth control, or deliberate prevention of a pregnancy. Common forms of contraception include condoms, diaphragms, and birth control pills.

CUSTODY AGREEMENT: a legal agreement about who has the right to take care of a child

HETEROSEXUAL: a person who is physically attracted to members of the opposite sex

HOMOPHOBIA: fear or dislike of homosexuals

HOMOSEXUAL: a person who is physically attracted to members of the same sex

INCEST: sexual abuse that occurs within the family

I STATEMENT: a statement that begins with the word *I*, such as, "I feel bad when you cancel plans with me to hang out with your friends from the hockey team instead."

ROHYPNOL: a preparation of a drug formally known as flunitrazepam. It can cause people to lose consciousness or become confused and is sometimes used by rapists to take sexual advantage of victims. Rohypnol is also known as roofies, or the date rape drug.

SELF-IMAGE: a kind of mental picture we have of ourselves, including how we look and act

SEXUAL ORIENTATION: a person's attraction toward other people, whether of the opposite sex, the same sex, or both sexes

SEXUALLY TRANSMITTED DISEASE: any of various diseases or infections that can be transmitted by sexual contact

TRANSGENDERED: a word to describe a biological male who feels female or a biological female who feels male

SOURCE NOTES

13 Ry Russo-Young, quoted in Susan Dominus, "Growing Up with Mom & Mom,"
    New York Times, October 24, 2004, http://query.nytimes.com/gst/fullpage
    .html?res=9903E0DC123AF937A15753C1A9629C8B63&pagewanted=1
    (April 4, 2011).
13 Ibid.

SELECTED BIBLIOGRAPHY

Centers for Disease Control and Prevention. "Talk to Teens about Healthy
    Relationships." CDC. February 22, 2011.
    http://www.cdc.gov/features/chooserespect (April 21, 2011).
Federal Trade Commission: Facts for Consumers. "Social Networking Sites:
    Safety Tips for Tweens and Teens." May 2006.
    http://www.ftc.gov/bcp/edu/pubs/consumer/tech/tec14.shtm (April 21,
    2011).
Nelson, Noelle C. *Dangerous Relationships: How to Identify and Respond to the
    Seven Warning Signs of a Troubled Relationship*. Cambridge, MA: Perseus
    Publishing, 1997.
Palo Alto Medical Foundation. "Eight Things to Do to Practice Better
    Communication." 2011.
    http://www.pamf.org/teen/abc/buildingblocks/eightthings.html (April 21,
    2011).
Pransky, George S. *The Relationship Handbook*. LaConner, WA: Pransky &
    Associates, 2001.
Psychology Today. "Are You Dating an Abuser?" December 17, 2008.
    http://www.psychologytoday.com/blog/anger-in-the-age-
    entitlement/200812/are-you-dating-abuser (April 21, 2011).
Roberts, Anita. *Safe Teen*. Vancouver, CA: Polestar, 2001.
Rosenberg, Marshall B. *Nonviolent Communication: A Language of Life*. Encinitas,
    CA: Puddle Dancer Press, 2003.
Segal, Jeanne. *The Language of Emotional Intelligence: The Five Essential Tools
    for Building Powerful and Effective Relationships*. New York: McGraw-Hill,
    2008.
Weeks, Dudley. *The Eight Essential Steps to Conflict Resolution*. New York:
    Tarcher, 1994.

FURTHER READING

Center for Young Women's Health
http://www.youngwomenshealth.org
This useful website provides carefully researched health and relationship
information for teen girls.

Doeden, Matt. *Conflict Resolution Smarts: How to Communicate, Negotiate,
Compromise, and More*. Minneapolis: Twenty-First Century Books, 2012.
Learn more about how to successfully manage and resolve conflicts in this
helpful selection.

Golus, Carrie. *Take a Stand! What You Can Do about Bullying*. Minneapolis: Lerner
Publications Company, 2009. Read all about bullying, a common and toxic
relationship problem that affects many teens.

Harris, Ashley Rae. *Cliques, Crushes, & True Friends: Developing Healthy
Relationships*. Edina, MN: Abdo, 2009. This title blends fictional narrative
with advice from a licensed psychologist on topics ranging from cliques to
peer pressure to dating.

———. *Is This Really My Family? Relating to Your Relatives*. Edina, MN: Abdo,
2009. Fictional stories and tips from a psychologist help teens cope with
challenging family situations.

Hasler, Nikol. *Sex: A Book for Teens*. San Francisco: Zest Books, 2010.
This funny, frank book covers everything readers want to know about
teenage sexuality.

Social Networking Sites: Safety Tips for Tweens and Teens
http://www.ftc.gov/bcp/edu/pubs/consumer/tech/tec14.shtm
This page offers lots of excellent safety tips on using social networking
sites.

Stay Teen
http://www.stayteen.org
This site features useful information about sex and preventing unplanned
pregnancies.

Teen Relationships
http://www.teenrelationships.org
Visit this site for information on healthy romantic relationships and recognizing signs of an abusive relationship. You'll also find a quiz to test whether your relationship is healthy.

TeensHealth
http://kidshealth.org/teen
Check out this site for information on relationships, body-image issues, emotions, families, sexual health, and more.

Yancey, Diane. *STDs*. Minneapolis: Twenty-First Century Books, 2012. Find out more about what STDs are and how you can prevent them.

Young Men's Health
http://www.youngmenshealthsite.org
This site for teen boys features interesting topics ranging from emotional health to sexuality.

LERNER
e
SOURCE

Expand learning beyond the printed book. Download free, complementary educational resources for this book from our website, www.lerneresource.com.

INDEX

abuse, 49–57

birth control, 43
breakups, 47
bullying, 21–23, 36–37, 39, 46, 51

casual relationships, 14
cliques, 36–37, 39–40
communication, 25–26
conflict, 38
cyberbullying, 21–23, 54

dating, 40–42
divorce, 12

family relationships, 10–13, 32–34
friendships, 14, 34–40

homosexuality, 12–13, 46

Internet safety, 20–21

meeting people, 17–21, 24–25

peer pressure, 34–36

rape, 52
romantic relationships, 15, 40–47,
    54–55

self-image, 28–29
sex, 42–45, 50, 52
sexual orientation, 46
sexually transmitted diseases, 43
siblings, 11
social networking websites, 19,
    22–23, 54

ABOUT THE AUTHOR

Joyce Markovics has been writing and editing books on topics ranging from bats to blizzards for the school and library market since 1998. She and her husband, Adam, live in New York City.